Markers on the Way to God:
God's Grace Transforming Mental Illness

Wendel L. Miser with
James S. Miser, MD

For more information about this title or to order other books
and/or electronic media, contact the publisher:

Atkins & Greenspan Publishing
TwoSistersWriting.com
18530 Mack Avenue, Suite 166
Grosse Pointe Farms, MI 48236

ISBN:
978-1-956879-28-5 (Hardcover)
978-1-956879-29-2 (Paperback)
978-1-956879-30-8 (eBook)

Printed in the United States of America

All the stories in this work are true.

Cover and Graphic Design: Van-garde Imagery, Inc.

Photo credit for author photos: Mary E. Miser

To all those who came to me with a gift
in their heart and the Good Book in their hand.

Contents

Foreword

It has been a privilege to write and edit this book with Wendel, in addition to his previous book, *A Valiant Battle: A Journey with Schizophrenia*. In the writing, we have grown closer as brothers and as brothers in Christ. *A Valiant Battle* not only tells of his healing from schizophrenia, but also describes his spiritual journey. These journeys to healing and wholeness are remarkable and are a testimony to the healing power of a loving God. At times, writing Wendel's story with him has been emotional and challenging as I have reflected on his experience.

This book, *Markers on the Way to God*, tells Wendel's story in his own poetry and prose. The text presents his thoughts and emotions as he dealt with schizophrenia and later as he reflects on his healing from this condition. It also describes the importance of his faith to his physical healing. This healing, based in his relationship with Christ, demonstrates the importance of a holistic understanding of healing and the greatness of our God.

— James S. Miser, MD

Introduction

OVER MANY YEARS AND in many ways, these pages have become my witness to God's Word telling of my salvation through the living Christ. What is written on these pages in poetry and prose is also my witness to the power and the beauty of the message of Christianity. It is the story of one man's faith telling of the living hope in the sacrifice of Christ on the cross and of the new life that comes from His resurrection that has become true for me.

My Faith

The joy I find in Jesus is profound: a joy that is life-sustaining, evidenced by the hope, love, and grace embodied in Jesus' sacrifice for us all. My heart sings of a new freedom given to me by His loving act on the cross that has released me from years of imprisonment by a disease marked by anxiety and instability.

Once lost in the grip of schizophrenia, I am now in the hand of Jesus and the household of God. Many years ago, I asked the Lord into my life after realizing that I needed him terribly and having nowhere else to go. By doing so, I found that one prayerful knock at the door to eternal life changed my life forever. Years have passed since that time. I know now that I have become an adopted son of my Heavenly Father. My repentant knock on that door opened to me the realization of my need for the saving grace of the Lord Jesus Christ. What followed was the reality of my being born again as a child of God through what Jesus had done for me on the cross and the importance of my relationship with God through Christ.

The beauty of Christ's birth, the agony of his death on the cross, and his resurrection are God's plan to overcome sin. Jesus obeyed his Father and went to the cross. By this merciful act, Jesus brought me into a right relationship with my Heavenly Father. On the cross, Jesus substituted himself for me, paid the penalty for my sin by dying there (John 3:16-17), and is at the right hand of the Father, eternally resurrected.

Later in my life, the resurrected Jesus bestowed the Holy Spirit upon me. I now have sure knowledge that God is with me always. By being sealed with the Holy Spirit, I came to know the possibility of the resurrection of my own life as I follow Jesus. True life is the

Holy transformation of life to the spiritual. True life is eternal life lived out in the present and is of the Spirit given by God lived out in the flesh. This is true life lived before the living God.

Writing

During the years I sang with the National Men's Chorus in the Washington D.C. metro area beginning in 1999, I once borrowed a pen from a fellow singer. As he gave it to me, he said: "Make sure you write something good with it." Around that time, I realized that my relationship with Jesus would be important when I detect that others need Him and that I may be the only one who can teach them about Him. In this volume, it is my hope that I have written well of Jesus and the Heavenly Father.

My Coming Out of Darkness

The Hill

The hill I have been climbing has become level.

The fog I have been in has lifted.

After running for a while, I have slowed to a walk.

I have struggled but now accepted.

The turmoil inside has begun to quiet.

Love has pushed back fear,

And the door to a heart is opening.

In clear voice, a promise has been given.

I know now my tears will be caught.

My hope will be answered.

Where I Suffered the Most

Where I had suffered the most
Jesus put His cross.
It has relieved
The pain of years not knowing the
Grace and peace only He can give.

In the beginning was a stark realization of life,
Not knowing where to turn.
Eye and ear gave no answer.
The interior realm not yet searched,
Discovery and divine disclosures
Yet to be made.

Existence seemed to have
No sense of the Holy.
Forgotten was the love I had
Known as a child.
Silent noise resounded within.

And yet, in the middle of it, the Lord
Was with me in prayer and in His Word.
What to make of it, my reason no longer adequate.

Now, a life of praise to the one who put His cross
Where I had suffered the most.
The pain there transformed to a love that
Knows His grace and eternal peace.

If the Lord Meant

If the Lord meant me to be saddled with my disease, I am very glad that I went through the psychotic episode that preceded it. For I know that this experience has led, with therapy, to a rewarding journey filled with faith in God, courage to face the challenges of life, a profound love for family and friends who offered encouragement and hope for life's possibilities, a commitment to health and to staying true to myself, and my acceptance of my responsibility for navigating the long road of life.

Into My Wilderness

You have followed me into my wilderness,
Lord, so you are there when I turn around.
You lead me out of that wilderness with a loving
Hold that brings me home to you. It is only then
That my realization of your presence with me
Becomes unmistakable. My understanding,
Then, is born of what I need.
Within your love comes my strength.
Why? Because in your Word, I am your
Child whom You have created after your Son,
Jesus, an heir to your throne.

Anxiety

An anxiety condition has been
The journey to meaning.
Once realized, it can now stop.
Slowing to an understanding of why
And acceptance of its necessity.
Living through its induced confusion
Only to find a light of a different kind;
One that bids welcome to the anxious soul.
A light that gives healing a place, a time, and a context
To allow growth past its reality.
Hope—the growth, and Love—the
Balm for the wound.
Why is not the question.
Why not is the answer given under
The light of providence.
Meaning given dignity and purpose.
A life burgeoning to joy.
Faith born out to its author
And his way.
Resting in the hand of the one
Who knew that anxiety would come to meaning
And meaning would be the gift.

Dear Friend,

When I was a boy, I heard of a man called Jesus from another time and place who was both loving and forgiving to everyone he met. I paid attention to the stories of him and learned of his example and teaching.

As I grew, his time and place were replaced with my own and I forgot about his loving and forgiving way. By the time I was a young man, my ways were important to me and I paid attention to my concerns, my time, and my story.

As time passed, my strength for my own life and concern, as well as my own self and place, became weak and strained from consideration of my own affairs.

My road to my own desire grew weary and I grew tired of it.

One day, I fell to the ground in exhaustion and confusion.

Shortly thereafter, a stranger, twice my age, whom I will call Peter, came upon me on the ground and helped me up to rest for a moment. Peter reminded me of this man called Jesus who was both loving and forgiving to everyone.

After resting with me a while, he helped me up and we walked down the path I had been on. As we walked, he spoke of this man, Jesus, of his example and of his teaching. At once, I saw an image of Jesus reflected in Peter. I asked Peter:

"How did you come to great discernment about this man, Jesus?"

He said to me: "As I grew from childhood, my concern for my own affairs eventually clouded my consideration of this man. I grew lonely on my own road. I was about your age when I was helped up by another after a fall I took after rushing about my worldly affairs. On that day, this wonderful man whose name was Paul assured me of this Jesus from another time and place. He reminded me of his love and compassion, of his example and his teaching. He prayed for me and gave me a Holy book. From reading the book, I remembered the Jesus I had learned of as a child. I studied and learned of his will and way. I discovered a faith, hope, and love far stronger than I had known before. And I learned why his Father sent him to earth.

"As I grew, I dropped my concern for myself and began to search for a way to follow him and his example. Along the way, I have found many who have dropped to the ground due to exhaustion from selfish pursuit. Let me help you! I will pray for you now and you may have the book of Jesus and his word that Paul gave me many years ago. Go, search, and follow him helping others who fall."

With that, we parted ways. It has been many years since my fall. I have studied and learned myself from Peter's Holy book. I continue to pray. If you fall, I will help you up, walk with you and tell of this man Jesus, from another time and place.

An Experience of God

It has taken many years for me to have
An experience of God. To see and
Experience my God. To realize that He loves me,
And by that love I can love others. That he wants me to
Know him and have a relationship with him in a way
That I no longer imprison myself in my anxiety and
Fear of what tomorrow may bring, but rather,
Live in joyful anticipation of a future
Embraced by Him.

I am amazed that I am here, but not surprised
Why it took so long, I didn't know and
Couldn't have known. Until now.

I now know that He is always faithful and
That His faithfulness encompasses every
Realm of my life in Him. I now realize that I have an essential
Relationship with Him that cannot be broken by any power
Known or unknown. I now realize that having a
Relationship with Him will open deeper relationships with
Others.

Faith, love, and hope all have meaning now
That lend perspective for my life that I will
Live in the knowledge that all is well.
But by the grace of God go I with the absolute
Knowledge that He cares for me absolutely
And that He is always and will forever be with me.

Live Eternally

In the following memoir, I remember how it was for me long ago when I turned to Jesus after realizing I was suffering with mental illness. At the time, the outward expression of my life was unsettling and inwardly more than confusing. I am very grateful for the love of Mary, good doctors and their medicine in this journey. I wrote this in reflection, speaking of my own early experience and realization of Jesus' way. The inward relief was immediate, and my joy has lasted a lifetime. I wonder if you might hear your early experience as well.

I am in the wilderness of my life. I have been at a place in my life where nothing was working for me. Even here, I have been hearing about this Jesus for a long time, yet I am still wandering. One morning, I awake and sense for myself that the time has arrived. For the first time in my life, I perceive that I need to repent in the manner that the Jesus of history had foretold. I know I need to knock at His door. After some consideration, I do so, asking forgiveness in simple prayer.

After some time, I realize something's different. A flood of God's love comes over me in the Spirit of this Jesus—my conclusion: the door must be open. I feel supported. I feel lighter and I perceive a buoyancy of new joy. I feel that I am traveling with new spirit, with someone who is protecting me; I am not alone on the inside. I feel carried. As I begin to risk putting my burdens down, I pick up the Holy book and feel I can rest in the arms of spirit, love, and stillness. My sense of being rushed by the world's ways begins to subside; I can take a deep breath in a moment of refreshment while reading God's word.

The love of God and way of Jesus introduce me to grace. I begin to see the beauty of creation more clearly as the ways of the world fade. My body reacts with the release of tension, anxiety, and fear. I feel quietly responsive to the creation around me. I start to think anew. Even of new possibilities of approach. Emmanuel is with me, and I know He is there to hear my prayer; to steady me; to comfort me.

I feel excited by the joy I have found. Inwardly, with my companion in spirit, I am two as one. I feel emboldened for the first time. I start to speak from Jesus' perspective about the love of neighbor and the Father. The Spirit of Jesus gives me access to His Father's Kingdom—all because I feel His profound love. I knocked at His door, and He answered as he said he would. Jesus now walks with me in a way that tells me He has my back. When I trust Jesus, I realize God has wiped out my transgressions for His own sake. My sincere need for Jesus cements my restored relationship with God forever. I can breathe, stand up straight, be honest, have courage, and love myself as I spread Jesus' spirit into the world.

Jesus loves me. He always has and always will. He wants to give me the life He has always wanted for me in a way that I will realize my place in His Father's plan, in His Father's Kingdom, and in His Father's eternal safety. I am not surprised that I begin to feel separate from the affairs of the world, yet able to enter in a way to have an effective voice concerning them.

I am separate. I am new. I am effective. I have a voice. Perspective is gained about all kinds of things. My life begins to work—all because of my willingness to repent and knock. It's good news for the world. And it's good news for eternity. Jesus knew His time on the cross would be worth it. By His crucifixion and resurrection, I am being recreated. These are His gifts to me.

My life is before me under the light of God's eternal providence. So I go ahead and live eternally.

A Corner of Fear

I was blown by the winds of this world into a corner of fear, only to turn around to witness a cornerstone, the foundation of true life, the living hope where fear disappears to a life of love championed among people by the living God.

Leaving Ninety-Nine

I was so dreadfully lost and in my darkened desperation, I went to search for Jesus. In a moment's prayer, I cried to Him. As I searched, to my surprise, He came to me. In His light, my eye recognized Him. And I found that I had not only been found in His overwhelming grace, but that He had set me on His Father's foundation of steadfast love even before I was born. In that moment, I realized that I had never been lost from His eye; only from my own, causing me not to trust He was there.

My Reflections on the Word of God

The Love of God

The House of the Lord

Living in the house built by the Lord.

A key to every door.

Rooms with no walls.

Celestial ceilings

Painted with the color of life

And patterns of peace brushed

With everlasting grace.

His Son, the master window

To the Father's master plan

For the house large enough for all

Who will turn to him and trust His ways.

His love, the light expelling the dark

From every corner illuminating a forgiving space

For the living of every wounded soul;

Wounded from years spent within

Perceived walls of mind and body.

Love strong enough to free the eye and ear

To recognize the purpose of His shelter

From healing to wholeness.

Walking from room to room,

Each with its prayerful sounds

Of assurance and mercy.

A welcome sign of eternal hope stands
At the front door of this, his everlasting home.
All invited to enter by a savior who went to a cross
In its front yard to redeem all who enter.
His Father knew its price and method of payment
He loved us for its building.
A holy book has directions to it free of charge.
It will tell you of the way, the truth, and the life
For you in the house of your dreams.
Living in this house built by the Lord
A key to every door.
A resting place for every heart needing mercy.
Won't you knock at its front door?
Ring the doorbell with a prayer
Asking forgiveness of sin.
And don't be surprised if your Father
Opens the house to you as if
You and He are the only two
Who dwell within.

Becoming, Yet Unfinished

All of us are becoming. Yet in God's realm, we remain unfinished. Some of us will become unfinished symphonies on His behalf. Some will become unfinished Christmas carols for Him and some only notes on a page. We are becoming the music we learn from God embracing us within the rhythm of the beat of His heart for others to learn of our relationship with Him. His love is the instrument that plays the music for others to discover our kindness and care for them.

We all are becoming, but remain unfinished in the work of God's music, in service to Him on His composer's page. From a few simple notes woven in symphonic sound, we stand together as one for His band of Angels to transform the sound for Heaven's purpose here on earth. Unfinished though we are, one to another, we are becoming the music of God through the love we show to others.

Our Heavenly Father's Plan

The genius of our Heavenly Father's plan for our lives has been given to us through His Son, His example and life—by way of miracle, parable, prayer, and sacrifice. His Son has gifted us the Father by His cross. And the resurrected Jesus has gifted us the Holy Spirit from Heaven.

Our Heavenly Father's plan is for us to live in communion with all in Heaven and on earth in peace and grace all the days of our lives if we but follow Jesus.

In the Midst of Blessing

The brightest of lights has overcome darkness,
A resurrected life has overcome death,
An unconditional love has overcome hate,
An undying hope has overcome despair.
Incomprehensible grace is before us
For a faith in a future held by our Heavenly Father
For the joy of the living of our days.
We are in the midst of blessing
For what has been overcome.
Sin no longer has dominion over us
As we live within the gift of the Holy Spirit.
So, as we experience the gifts of the Father
Through His Son of Light, Love, Life, Hope, Grace,
Joy, they are ours as the Father wants
Them to be a blessing for our lives.

No Vacancy

When I encounter a "No Vacancy" sign
At the hotel and remember the little one when there
Was no room in the Inn, I
Find rest in the house He built.

Over and Above

Over and above and around this globe
Of ours is a loving God whose sole purpose
Has been to bring us back to the
Astounding realization that He is here for
Us and that He wants to have a relationship
With us where He has the controlling interest
In our lives so that His love is shared upon this
Earth among all of us. It took the cross of His
Son for us to recognize the magnitude and
The nature of His love and it is up to us to
Develop such a profound relationship with
Our God through prayer that we are able
To give others the gift without, ourselves,
Ever forgetting its price.

Let There Be

Let there be no mistake.
Our Heavenly Father and His Son are a
Permanence upon the horizon of our future
In this world. Trust as you look to them in
Every imaginable need as you live out your days.

Reconciliation

The gift of our freedom and new life
By our reconciliation to a Father's love is
Through substitution, resurrection,
And the descent of the Holy Spirit.

Genuine Relationships

Your relationship with Jesus is built
From the ground up on the foundation
Of the love of God. Love others on that
Basis and genuine relationships will flourish.

Release

The feeling of Joy is proportional
To the feeling of God's release from burden.
God's forgiveness is the assurance
Of the release. The one who is released
From burden can relax; take a deep breath
And breathe. The joy will carry him to
Thankfulness. The joy will cement a new
Relationship of reconciliation
And partnership between the two, to be sure.
God's forgiveness is complete.

'Tis a Gift

Romans 5:1-5 tells us: "1 Therefore being justified by faith, we have peace with God through our Lord Jesus Christ: 2 By whom also we have access by faith into this grace wherein we stand, and rejoice in hope of the glory of God. 3 And not only so, but we glory in tribulations also: knowing that tribulation worketh patience; 4 And patience, experience; and experience, hope: 5 And hope maketh not ashamed; because the love of God is shed abroad in our hearts by the Holy Ghost which is given unto us."

Long ago, at the heralding of a King by Gabriel's cry, our Heavenly Father showered His great mercy and love upon the earth with the birth of His Son: a Savior whose birth signaled God's intention to bring men away from sin and despair to redemption and forgiveness. We are now blessed with the limitless nature of that love and mercy shown to us by the cross Christ chose to bear—our Holy citizenship to gain with a right relationship with our God to nurture and sustain. We now travel following our Risen Lord with purpose, dignity, and excitement.

Our days are embedded in God's grace. We should never live and act without knowledge of that fact. We remember our companion as we break bread for truth and life. Remembering our companion surprises us to seek and to believe, provokes us to love God and neighbor, and in realizing true hope, we walk by faith beside Him to bring grace and peace to the world. Our wounds are healed by this Wounded Healer; our weaknesses are brought to endurance by this One who endured the cross; and our despair and sadness are brought to profound joy in this Resurrected One. Our redemption is by His act. Our new life is by His rising.

We are set in the valley of love and delight where He has bestowed the Holy Spirit upon us and eternal life is before us. A river of history runs through this valley flowing ceaselessly home to that long ago Easter morning upon which the resurrection of Jesus proclaimed that His rising has conquered Death in eternal victory dispelling its shadow for us there. In this valley, we will fear no evil.

It is our realization of these holy gifts that fill us with boundless joy, thankfulness, and prayer this day and forevermore.

True Joy

True joy comes from God.
Even in the experience
Of suffering,
To rise and experience the glory of God.

But One

Where Creator and creature
Are: not two, but one.

Profound Scientific Explanations

Profound scientific explanations only
Enhance our revelation of the
Existence of God.

Dear God

You gave us your Son from your
Timeless realm by virgin birth into
Time, for a time, to teach us that
Your eternal Spirit is granted to us.
The timely presence of your Son
Here on earth, your timeless
Gift of your Son's cross and your
Granting of the Holy Spirit frees us to
Walk as He did in our own time
With the knowledge that your
Eternal Spirit is with us.
With that Spirit, we, too, are
New creatures with your eternal in
Our living in the newness
Of life imparted to us by His
Resurrection and return to your
Right side. And it is your eternal realm
To which we are destined to go
From our time to be with You.

Redemption

God knows a present world torn by sin,
Despair, doubt, separation, anxiety, and
Loneliness is no place for His children.
God wants us home. And long ago, God
Acted on His promise to bring us home
For good. The Old Testament prophets
Foretold this. Redemption was that promise.
And the gift of His Son's cross was its
Fulfillment. Redemption is God's gift
And God's answered prayer to
Us for our return home to Him. This gift has
Inspired thankful adoration and praise
Beyond measure in the hearts of His
Children since its occurrence 2000 years ago.

For a Time

For a time, we are given all of Creation.
For all of eternity, we are given its Creator.

Why Rely?

Why rely on the human eye that can be plucked
Or the fleshly ear that can be silenced?
But rather, the inner eye that is silent and free
To see and know God in His Holy Spirit,
Or the inner ear that can recognize and listen
To our Heavenly Father when His
Voice appears.

He Does Not Hide

Our Heavenly Father does not hide from us. On the contrary, He sent His Son to earth so many years ago for us to see His sacrifice and by it, for us to learn and come to know our Heavenly Father through His Son. Our Heavenly Father wants our focus to be on Him. His design is for us to come to know Him while He offers protection from a world's future we cannot see. Our God veiled the future of this world so that we would come to rely on Him.

My Heavenly Father

My mind, released from years
Of imprisoned logic, is
Free to see Jesus
And know the Living God.

As God First Loved Us

God first loved us unconditionally.

He continues to do so and

We find ourselves in an ocean of His love.

Because of this, we spontaneously return our love to Him.

He asks us to love our neighbor as ourselves.

His love for us makes us

Able to love our neighbor as God intended.

In the process, we find our ability to love God.

Created and Then Created Anew

Through God's act of creation and

Jesus' act of redemption, we are created

And then created anew.

The God of All Time

The God of all time and the God of this time and the God of every time loves us now and forevermore. He is forever with us to guide us in this world. He is with us in the present moment and will always be with us through all time. Team up with God and your path through time will be full of grace and peace.

How I Love Thee

All the days of my life were written
In your book before I was a day old.
Oh my God, my God, how I love thee
Because you first loved me.

God Loves Them

God is weeping, yet
Smiles upon this earth.
He knows what has been done
Through His Son for His people.
He is reaching for His people
And bringing them home to Himself
Setting their heart ablaze with
His love that has no end.
God loves them for their saving.
Only God could ordain the gift.

Jesus and His Love for Us

Walking

Forgiven, I now walk down a road beside Jesus,
Guided by His steps, stepping for me.
I marvel at the grace and peace
He brings in the midst of
The hustle and bustle of
Today's world.
He is
The
Protection
I seek. He is the
Love I have needed.
With Jesus beside me,
Whom shall I fear?

Loving Me as I Am

Thank you, Lord, for loving me as I am.
It is now that I see.
Amazed, in spite of myself,
Of the precious grace with which
You surround me to keep me
Safe with you.

Behold This Man

Behold this man, this Jesus
For He is the Son of God,
Resurrected,
Resurrecting men to serve
His Father and His
Loving way.
The life of love unconditional
Redeeming mankind
For His purposes,
Each life found
To newness, purpose
And faith.

The Blueprint

Our relationship with Jesus gives us
The insight to see that God loved us first
So that we might learn to love others based
On the blueprint of His love for us.

Jesus Will Bring Us Home to Our Father

Jesus, the Heavenly Son,
Points to the Father who welcomes us home.
Jesus' way will mend us so that we
Will hear Him say, "Your faith has made
You well and all you do will be for
The glory of the Father."
Jesus knows our need for His Father's mercy.
It will keep us humble. Knowing that
We can always turn to our Father will
Keep us joyful.
The Father will not forsake us
And for that, we will be steadfast.
Jesus' way will teach us
The way for us to go and
His hold on us will be firm but gentle.
In walking with Jesus, we will find a song in our heart
Which we will sing in thankfulness to Him
Who brought us home to our Father.

Details

Jesus is in the details of ordinary life and, also, in the broad strokes of the wonder of it. Details of the ordinary and the wonder of the extraordinary cause us to thank God for His Son. Who else, if we go to Him in prayer, can smooth out the wrinkles of life and cause us to be amazed at the extraordinary. We are truly blessed that He is with us in a grace-full relationship where the details of the ordinary won't confound us and the extraordinary won't overwhelm us. In such a relationship, He gives us them both together in such a way that allows us to understand His hold on us in the smallest of detail simultaneously with the greatest expression of His miracle given to us in the moments of our lives.

Invited by a Babe

Invited by a babe from outside history,

We are asked to be in the world

But not of it

To welcome strangers,

To turn the other cheek,

To love our enemies,

To offer comfort to the afflicted

And the forgotten.

We point to the saving way of life:

The Way, the Truth, and the Life

Of the One who went to a cross

As our substitute for our sin to forgive us,

To free us, and to establish aright our

Relationship with our Heavenly Father.

Jesus went from manger to cross

Through tomb and beyond

For us to be freed in service

To those in need in His name.

A Bright Light Over Bethlehem

At the coming of the Lord, there was a bright light over Bethlehem. It was no match for the light of the manger. This manger light which all had witnessed is the light of the world. This spiritual light of Jesus is eternal in the bosom of men.

Through Jesus, such light changes men and brings them into the truth, properly focusing them on the works of the Lord and their Heavenly Father.

Epicenter of Grace

This Jesus, who is the center of grace,
Cornerstone of peace,
And fountain of love,
Offers to us an outstretched hand of hope
For steadfast faith on our journey
With the Heavenly Father who is
The only One who knows why we would
Come along with His Son on this lovely ride.

Jesus Is Beyond

Jesus is beyond the shadow of doubt,
The faith of the Holy Spirit tells me so.
Jesus is beyond the shadow of death.
Death is nothing but a shadow,
The faith in the resurrection tells me so.
Jesus is beyond in heaven
Yet with me, here,
My faith tells me that I, too, am beyond
In His care.
Jesus and I, not of this world.
Jesus, from outside history, came
Down to claim my soul.
I walk this valley with Him,
The faith of His presence tells me so.
Crucifixion nails could not hold Him
From an empty tomb to depart.
My recognition of Him in my being
Gives newness and rebirth to my life.
The babe in the manger to praise
For what His Father's purpose was
In sending Him.
Isaiah foretelling the promise of my
Redemption in His cross:
The life of Jesus given to me
So I may live for Him.
Reality is marked by His

Manger, cross, and tomb
For you and me
To give witness to His unconditional love
And immeasurable grace for us.
The fullness of their meaning is
Beyond our comprehension yet our faith
In Jesus' embrace tells us that our believing is knowing—
Knowing that He is here;
Knowing that He is beyond at the right hand
Of His Father yet near to us for us to see
That He is the way, the truth, and the life.

Lifeline

Jesus is our lifeline to our Heavenly Father who loves us unconditionally. This lifeline has no strings attached and its strength is
made of God's love tying us fast to our Father by an everlasting
knot. Our Father anchors us at one end and Jesus, at the other, is
holding us by the hand to steady us.

By this lifeline, we cannot be separated from God's love because
the length of its tether is unlimited.

At Hand

My relationship with Jesus will keep me mindful
That the Kingdom of God is at hand.

Clothed with Christ

If I am clothed in Christ,
Should I not speak from his perspective?

Manger Light

The glow of it
Will soften and warm the heart of the one
Who will search his relation to the babe
Lying there. Pardon, the assurance
And the gift given from what
Came to be.

For us, looking back to this Heavenly
Ordained birth gives promise
To the miracle of our own rebirth as
His holy presence returns us to holiness.

Bethlehem's star gave light
To the wise men on the way
To the manger.

Manger light gives a glow to hearts
On the way through cross and tomb,
Resurrection light to find.

Once found, perceptions change;
Manger light is as bright as resurrection
Light at the moment of its realizing;

Ponder this life that God gave to
Us in manger light,
Won't you?

You may find that the light of your rebirth
Is as bright as God intended
It to be.

The Lord's Pasture

The Lord's pasture includes sheep of all size and shape

Who graze upon grass of His landscape

Where there are no fences so as to confine

Nor rules that hold them in straight line.

They are free to roam under the hand of the one

By whose love and mercy, their souls are won

And by whose cross, so shameless,

Where He has accepted their sin, so blameless,

To set aright their brotherhood.

He has magnified His Father's light

In their holy sight

For the good of the sheep

Who all graze and peacefully sleep.

The Manger Light

Manger light is brighter than the sun.
Looking directly at the sun will blind.
Looking directly at the baby Jesus
will cause me to see.
The sun casts its shadows.
Jesus is the light of the world
who causes me to see
where there is no shadow.

Baby Jesus shines His pure and
Holy light in the soul
so as to cause me to see His Father—
His Kingdom, and His love unconditional.

The sun is of this world,
the Son is not.
Come to where there is no shadow.
Come to manger light!
Look to Him and see!
Live by His reflection in His light
for He is the Light of lights.

Home

For mankind, a terrestrial sphere
Is his physical home among
Other spheres in ordered cosmic space.
His spiritual home
Is with God beyond all that.
His ability to live at home
Requires his attention beyond.

Comes to Rest

Flesh comes to rest with the Holy Spirit
And recognizes it for its home.
The Holy Spirit marries the soul with
Its Eternal indwelling the flesh
Which surpasses all understanding.

Merciful Light

The Light of the world
Came to pardon, heal, and renew.
The light of the world
Is merciful light.

Sinless Nature

The sinless nature of Jesus,
Who upon the cross took on
And destroyed the sin of man
Thereby, is the perfect medicine
To heal the man who has a past
Dotted with it.

So Amazing!

The Lord of life came into this world
In such a simple and wonderful way
For an amazing reason. During His lifetime,
He taught lessons through parables
And performed miracles that amazed
The multitudes. His death on the cross
Was an act of selflessness for our forgiveness.
Because of this, we are saved in such a way
Never to be separated from the love of the
Living God. The empty tomb, evidence
Of the resurrection of Jesus, amazes me still—
All to transform us from ordinary creatures
To extraordinary creatures who are reunited
With an awesome God and His Son
At His right hand. So amazing are the
Lord's saving grace, peace, and love
For all of mankind.

Standing The Test of Time

The amazing thing about Jesus is that
He chooses you. When you accept Him, your relationship
With Him will stand the test of time.

Teach

My relationship with Jesus will
Cause me to understand that others need Him
And I am to teach them that
He is here.

Under His Wing

Under His wing, Jesus gives me a new way
To be in this world. A way that is marked by
Thankfulness, compassion, and grace.
My hope for the future is embedded in my
Undying faith in Him who guides me there.
My steps are easy, my relationships are loving,
And my being is at peace. With Jesus at my side,
My faith carries me forward from one moment
To the next with a freedom only the Creator can give.
For this, celebration with the joy that is in Him
Lights my path toward the new day. Alleluia.

Are You Ready?

Are you ready to change the world?
A friend said to me.

I don't need to be,
I said.

It has already been changed.
Jesus has changed it
For us forever.

Not Knowing

Not knowing where you are being led,
Yet having confidence in the one who
Is leading.

He Is Here

He is here with me
Where He is, there is forgiveness, freely given.

Companionship

The love of Jesus will not allow me
To fall beyond the grace of God
And imparts to me
A boundless joy and an
Endless hope.

Winter

In the dead of Winter,
The warmth of a life appeared
On a bed of hay to give us
The Holy promise of love
Unconditional, to forgive
Us beyond imagining, and
To give us our rightful place
In the heart and hand of our
Heavenly Father who
Ordained all of this for us
By His Son's most gracious act of
Mercy and sacrifice.

Giving The Lord Praise

Giving the Lord praise
For a moment in time so confused
Only He would know
Its cause.
His purpose, to redeem the confusion
For His eternal moments to bless
As he imparts His
Understanding.

Wilderness

You have followed us into our wilderness, Lord,
So you are there when we turn around.
You lead us out of that wilderness with a
Loving hold that brings us home to you.
It is only then that our realization of your presence
With us becomes unmistakable.
Our understanding of you is born of what we need.
We search and our strength within your love is in
Our knowing. Why?
Because in your word, we are your children.
We are your creatures that are created
After and within the love your Son, Jesus,
Heirs to your throne.

Trusting the Lord

A good and excellent way is brought to those
Who trust the Lord even in those moments we
Question. We cannot foresee or fore know the future,
Though by faith we know that God has ordained it.
By His Word we know God and by faith we know
That He holds the future.

If Jesus Is in The Room

The light will shine.

The warmth can be felt.

Differences can be accepted.

Hope can blossom.

Love will surround.

Goodwill will spread.

The hungry will be fed.

Freedom is shared.

Faith is sustained.

Wrongs will be forgiven.

Grace will hold.

Pain will be healed.

Thankfulness will multiply.

Singing will be spontaneous.

Laughter will enliven.

Prayers will abound.

Compassion will engage.

Needs will be met.

The Father will be seen.

Courage will grow.

Problems will be solved.

There will be enough bread.

Loveliness will blossom.

Doubts will starve.

Attitudes will become healthy.

Darkness will be transformed.

Encouragement is offered.

The weak become strong.

The sick are made well.

Questions are answered.

Life is sustained.

Shadows will disappear.

The crooked will be made straight.

Peace will arrive.

Men will humble themselves.

Their wants will be curbed.

Vision will be gained.

Deafness will be overcome.

Longing hearts will find.

Understanding will heal.

Anxiety will rest.

Depression will subside.

Cures will be found.

Confidence will stand.

Relationships will flourish.

Children will be made whole.

Bitterness will end.

There will be a new tomorrow.

Fears will be vanquished.

Blessings will be counted.

Tensions will be calmed.

Hands will hold.

Promises will be kept.
And Spirit is bestowed.
Truth will be manifested.
Breathing will be easier.
The lie will be exposed.
Intentions will be forthright.
The way will be found.
His hand will protect.

New life is offered.
Paths are found.
Nothing will separate.
Restlessness will be calmed.
Honesty will be felt.
Anger will be dissolved.
Plans will be confirmed.
Death will be swallowed up.
And loving hearts will rest.

Larger Influence

Jesus gave Himself on a cross for our sake and when resurrected, He gave us the Holy Spirit and our ability to recognize our Heavenly Father and live with Him through that Spirit. The Lord is, for us, the largest influence in our lives. As we pray the prayer he taught us, we pray for God's will to be done, not ours. He tells us to love God with all our heart and love one another as ourselves. When we act in this way, we are helping God's children. And further, He asks us to help the least of these.

Remember, the Lord is the largest influence in our lives. Let Him influence you. He is asking us to respond with love to the needs of all His children.

We Will Be Changed

He's got the whole world in His hand and the Lord is the Lord of all. He is the Lord of all that concerns you. Within this context, give Him all that concerns you: all your problems, all your attention, all your love, all your prayer, all your hopes, all your effort, all your time, and all your devotion and see what happens. He will take care of all that concerns us. All of what concerns us will be transformed and we will be changed.

Where Our Treasure Is

Let us come to the Lord's Table

Remembering our Lord Jesus Christ.

On His cross at Calvary,

He mercifully made manifest

The love of God for all.

It is a love from which

We cannot be separated

Through Jesus Christ.

It speaks to us of our treasure in

Heaven, which for us is incorruptible.

We are to let earthly treasures go.

We know this truth as we turn

To Matthew's gospel which teaches

Us the nature of what our relationship

To God and our neighbor should be.

"Thou shalt love the Lord thy God, with all

Thy heart, and with all your soul, and with all

Thy mind…Thou shalt love thy neighbor

As yourself." (Matthew 22:37 and :39)

The treasure is here.

Jesus tells us that where our treasure

Is, our hearts will be also. So come

To where God's love is made manifest.

Come to where your heart wants to be.

And bring your neighbor.

The Nature of Jesus as Our Saving Grace

As I see it, God's purpose in sending his Son to earth was to save us from ourselves and return us to our Heavenly Father, the living God. Saving us from ourselves means saving us from our fallen conditions of weak and sinful behaviors. During His life, Jesus loved sinners and taught us about the preeminence of God's love in order to bring us back to a realization of God's hold on us.

The significance of our baptism is that we are baptized into his death only to rise to new life in God. In going to the cross, He obeyed the Heavenly Father on our behalf. The significance of His dying was that in his dying for us, He gave us complete forgiveness of our sins on earth. The significance of the open tomb three days later leading to His resurrection was that He gave us our first sense of eternal life on earth lived in and before God.

Through the incredible gift of the Holy Spirit, Jesus bestowed all of the gifts that are evidenced by His life, death and resurrection upon us. The Holy Spirit is a seal of these, God's gifts of His love and kingdom through Christ Jesus.

The apostle Paul grasped this image to describe the sealing of the Lord: "13 In whom ye also trusted, after that ye heard the word of truth, the gospel of your salvation: in whom also after that ye believed, ye were sealed with that Holy Spirit of promise, 14 Which is the earnest of our inheritance until the redemption of the purchased possession, unto the praise of his glory." (Ephesians 1:13-14)

Today, His bestowing of the Holy Spirit on believers comes as Jesus is resurrected in Heaven. God's Kingdom is not of this world! Eternal life is an expression of His Kingdom upon and within us.

Step Out of The Boat

Step out in faith from the boat. Do not be afraid. Jesus is here. His mercy will catch you and God's love will hold you. A friend said to me, "Stand still and see the salvation of the Lord."

Follow and give your will to Him. He will hold your burdens as you carry your cross. Pray to Him and He will listen and guide you. Step out of the boat. Jesus is here. He is close and He waits for you to trust Him.

In Listening to Jesus

In listening to Jesus, you will hear God's voice.
In listening to Jesus, you will come to know
God's heart and your own heart will be calmed.
In listening to Jesus, you will hear
God's song for you and humanity, a song
That is loving and sure.
In listening to Jesus, you will find rest.
In listening to Jesus, you will be compelled to be kind,
To seek justice, to be compassionate, and to be loving.
In listening to Jesus, you will be compelled to be strong
In the service of the less fortunate and hungry.
In listening to Jesus, you will look outward to a world that needs
you; and
In listening to Jesus, you will be able to accept
What you cannot do.

Crucifixion and Resurrection

By The Place

By the place where I sit, many pass.

How many come from manger light?

How many travel by the light of the Risen One?

And how many travel toward

The foot of the cross,

There to find heaven's gate

To eternal life?

Crossed-up

When you get double-crossed by life's circumstance,
Crossed up in finding your direction, or trouble crosses your path,
look to the one Who was up on the cross at Calvary for help.

The True Gift of Easter

The crucifixion of the Sinless One,
Broken in sorrow, mercifully assures us of
A holy and gracious new life in
A guaranteed and genuine relationship
With our Heavenly Father forevermore.
Our relationship is magnified
And glorified on Easter by the resurrection
Of our Lord who is alive with the Father
And through the Holy Spirit
Which He faithfully bestows upon us.

Discarded on a Tree

The babe in the manger
Became discarded on a tree
To make His Father's children
Heirs to His Father's glorious Kingdom.

Epitome

Jesus' act that He bore on a tree,
Signaling forgiveness for mankind,
Was the epitome of
God's grace toward us.

The Foundation

The foundation enabling a man to do his best was forged on a cross some two thousand years ago. By this most precious sacrifice, the Son of God has helped men reach the height of their ability to do good in the world. This achievement is not by the strength of men, but rather by their faith in this one who guides them through hardship, failure, desperation, doubt, and uncertainty to a place where their accomplishment is possible and, therefore, attainable.

The merit of the accomplishment stands relational to this foundation for all to see the good work. A man will flourish in his good and best work if he will but stand firm in this foundational reality.

In Another Time

In the history of another time,

The stone did roll away.

The door to the tomb is forever open.

The significance of this opened door

Can be fully experienced and understood

Only after a prayerful repentant knock on the door of

Another kind, that of eternal life.

This second door is a door which the Son of God will

Open to you if you will only do so.

The Risen Lord is waiting to teach you

His life-giving Spirit and the meaning

Of the stone that rolled away opening the tomb.

In the history of another time, the cross did stand holding

The one who now has left the tomb and

Has gone to the right hand of the Father.

In the history of today, knock, won't you? The

Risen one will teach you that the door that is forever

Open preceded the door upon which you will knock.

This is true so you can be at home with the One

Who promises eternal life to you

So that you find abundant true life in Him.

What Jesus Did for Us

For all our transgressions before God, Jesus did for us what we could not do for ourselves. He took our place on the cross of shame. Jesus gave us the Father's relationship through what he had done. It is through our brother, Jesus, that we live unto the Father as newly adopted children in his Kingdom. The Risen Son is alive in God's Kingdom and so are we.

Intersection of Love and Sin

Christ's crucifixion is at the crossroads of God's unconditional love for us and our immense shameful condition as sinners in the history of mankind. If His Son's cross influences you at all, as God has set His road before you, you will know that the road straight ahead of you is draped with His love.

Go forward with Jesus at your side and cross over that road of sin. Your life will turn to joy.

On His Cross

Jesus on His cross.

Love holding Him there for me.

Knowing He would rise,

To save and protect.

That was His purpose.

Suffering, He knew I would learn

Of His grace.

Yet so hard to convince others.

He knew I would carry His message

To a world confused

By God's divine love,

A love that knows heavenly peace.

A Son born to go to the cross

Chose me to proclaim His word.

So powerful yet so precious

To move a mountain of sin.

I know He is with me to guide,

To teach others that He is here

To love, to save a world

from sin and death.

Resurrected Spirit

The essence of the resurrection of Jesus
Filled the open tomb after its occurrence
And now fills the world, universe, heavens,
Heaven, and ourselves through the Spirit.
There is now nowhere where the
Resurrected Spirit of Jesus is not.

Road to Emmaus

We are disciples on the road to Emmaus
With the realization of the presence of the
Risen Christ with us. We are traveling with
Renewed spirit, mind, and body. We step
Out to tell those along the way of the saving
Grace we find from His cross to His
Presence now with us. His love is the light
For our path as we are compelled to
Change our response to the human
Condition. His love sustains us as we
Stretch ourselves to new levels of
Sincerity, commitment, and honesty.

Road to His Cross

New life is found on our road to His cross at the crossroad
Of His story and ours in this, the history of our time.

When He Cried from The Cross

When he cried "it is finished" and died,
He ushered in our complete forgiveness
By God and our new relationship
With our Heavenly Father.

With Jesus

He has been given to you on the cross,

Your gift is displayed at the resurrection,

He waits for you to come home,

And if you don't, He searches for you as if you are the only one missing,

His countenance is bestowed upon you when you turn around,

The door is opened at your knocking,

The light appears when you recognize Him,

The storm passes when you finally trust,

Grace appears in your surrender,

Your path is cleared when you wait upon Him,

His answer comes when you pray,

His love stays with you as you walk with Him,

By your belief, you will realize you have been saved by His cross,

And your joy is made complete by His walking with you.

Emptiness

Have you ever felt empty
As an earthen vessel
When faced with:
The emptiness of feeling,
The emptiness of promise,
The emptiness of words?
Consider the fullness of the cross
And the emptiness of the tomb
In profoundly recognizing
The redeeming grace
Of our Lord, Jesus Christ.

The Magnitude

The resurrection of our Lord Jesus Christ
Demonstrates the sheer magnitude of the
Victory of his cross for us all. It demonstrates
The magnitude of the love He has for each of us
And the magnitude of the hope we are to have in Him.

Passing from Death to Life

We remember the Son
Affixed there to the cross while
We deny, we betray,
We doubt, we forsake,
We pierce.
We hammer in our fear
And then we run.
He struggles there, yet
He accepts, He forgives,
He loves.
We do not know what we do,
Yet he does.
He knows why He went there,
Obedient to the Father.

Eternal Life Is a Grace

Eternal life is God's grace that is conferred upon us
Here and now by Jesus' merciful act on the cross and resurrection.
Eternal life is the life we find ourselves in as we live out
Our lives. Because of God's grace, we have certain
Knowledge that we will be carried through
Death by His grace to be with Jesus
In His eternal realm.

More Love

Love

Love: given of God, from God.
It is He and He is here.

Love: come down from Heaven.
It is He and He is here.

Love: in a lowly manger.
It is He and He is here.

Love: lived among us.
It is He and He is here.

Love: scorned among men.
It is He and He is here.

Love: nailed to a cross.
It is He and He is here.

Love: laid in a tomb.
It is He and He is here.

Love: raised from the dead.
It is He and He is here.

Love: given as Spirit.
It is He and He is here.

Love: for us, with us.
It is He and He is here.

Love: It is He and He is here.
This Jesus.

Love's Hand

Love's hand has opened my eyes to the
Knowledge that they are open,
To the newness of what lies before,
Open to the knowledge of something
Completely changed,
Yea, the unlocking of a door.

My mind thirsts,
My heart sings full of joy unquenchable.
What couldn't be done before
Can now be done: the door is open,
Passage is guaranteed.
Love has opened my eyes.
My prayer of many years
Has been answered.

Love is Strongest

Love is strongest
When it forgives.

Love Song

The Lord of the dance
Makes my heart dance
To the music of His love song.

Love

The Lord Operating Victorious
In Each of us.

When All Else Fails

When all else fails, the love of God
Through His Son won't.

Grace Upon Grace

Grace upon grace,
Grace from the beginning, and grace forever.
Love so forgiving it enables a broken
Spirit to heal to new life.

Love Waited

Love waited for me to recognize it.
It then enveloped me as if my time
Prior to my recognition of it never existed.

Love, Life and Death

The following story was paraphrased from in a sermon given by the Reverend Jack Austin at First Christian Church in Falls Church, Virginia on Sunday, May 1, 2011.

On the day imminent Death arrived for my father's wife, in the room with them were Life and Love. At the appointed time, Death announced to the other two: "She's coming with me."

Life became stunned.

Love was quick to respond: "Oh no, she's not."

Surprised, puzzled, and scoffing nonetheless, Death responded: "Well, well." He asked Life: "What did you teach her?!"

Life replied: "As she grew with me, I taught her the need for Love's joy, hope, courage, faith, patience, compassion, and perseverance. And as for you, I taught her that when this day and time would come, you would have no sting for her."

Pondering, Death questioned Love: "What did you teach?"

Love said: "That I am patient and kind and rejoice with the truth; that I keep no record of wrongs; and that I bear all things and always trust; that I am eternal and will always be with her; and that I come with a cross of redemption for her repentant heart."

In that moment, in a profound panic, Death fled the room. Following, as Life knew the power of Love, Life said a quiet goodbye and left. Only Love remained holding her as she passed into its mystery.

---

* *Published with permission from Reverend Jack Austin.*

My Continuing Journey to Light

At The Nudging of a Friend

When I was younger, at the nudging of a friend,
I went off looking for Jesus. I did not know that
God has a grand view. While in God's hands, I
Looked and looked and looked.
God saw that I was looking for Jesus.
Once He knew I was looking for His Son,
He knew He would get my attention.
He let His children help me look for Him
And He picked His time for my attention-
Getting. He put in the sight of my eyes the
Figure on a cross of which I took notice.
God knew I would study its meaning and come
To know that I am found. And I tucked Jesus in
My heart ever since.

Collective Prayers

God's Kingdom and the will of God
Is and will continue to be present
In the world for us. We offer our
Collective prayers that we might know
His will for our lives.

Lead Us Heavenward

As we follow you up the hill of our lives, we know our steps will be guided by you through whatever we face. Our paths may be difficult, but we know you will always be there taking us ever higher as you hold us in God's grace. As we go, we also know that as we yearn to stay close to you, we will be able to leave our past and, trusting you, embrace our future in which, in the brightness of your light, we would dare to soar higher than we ever thought possible.

We thank you for your companionship, your guidance, and your direction. Lead us on, Jesus. Lead us Heavenward.

Listen at Rest

After everything has come to rest in stillness
And earthly murmurs cease, the Lord's
Voice can be distinguished from within
The enveloping silence.

Magnificence

A friend spoke of magnificence today,
The magnificence he sees in me
That reminds him of the Lord's hold on me.
I told him I feel the same of him.
When the Lord imparts magnificence,
You can feel it and see it in others.

This conversation has been going on between
The two of us for quite a while and
When I see my friend, I see his magnificence
And I feel mine.

I am not surprised for I know that it's the Lord's
Doing for both of us.

We laugh full of joy at our realization held by grace.

Divine love has sparked magnificence
Deep within us lifting our companionship
Ever higher.

Blessings of gladness and joy on my
Magnificent friend.
Let his light shine.

At The Center

There are many people who have helped me
With my illness over my years.
With my belief in and my thankfulness to Jesus,
I have tried to put Christ at the center
Of my life for this reason:
That their help may magnify and help me
Be of some help to others.

My Earthly Life

Somewhere in the framework of my earthly life
There is a cross to find, to accept, and to bear.
The cross then gives a Holy and divine
Dimension to that framework in which my life
Is lived by faith, in hope, and for love.
His grace is recognized and peacefully
Acknowledged. Eternal life is then perceived.

Passing Them Through

Heavenly angels watch over
Those who have struggled,
Passing them through tribulation
Keeping them nigh to the one
Who protects and loves them.
Saints know that in the years
That have preceded us
And who now hold company
With those same angels!

Surprise of Life

The surprise of life is what happens to you when you recognize the Son of God for the first time.

The surprise of life is what happens to you when you get to know the Heavenly Father about whom His Son tells you.

The surprise of life is what happens to you when you listen to the lifetime stories about the Son of God.

The surprise of life is what happens to you when you read the Bible and the Word of God jumps off the page and into your heart.

The surprise of life is what happens to you when you discover God's purpose for the cross of Christ.

The surprise of life is what happens to you when you discover the stone rolling away.

The surprise of life is what happens to you when God's Holy Spirit descends on you.

The surprise of life is what happens to you when you share with others the surprise of your life.

The surprise life is what happens to you when others respond to you because of the surprise of your life…

With Jesus, life remains a surprising gift!

Thankfulness

Thankfulness is a place to which you arrive after you have gone down all the wrong paths of your own desires, gotten lost or confused, lonely or angry and have, by chance, found people willing to steer your spirit back toward home with the winds of their love, compassion, hope, and grace. It's in their steering your spirit back to you in ways you recognize that your gratitude is born and blossoms.

Some do it by the light of the Holy Spirit, others by their courage, and still others by their commitment to you. It is your thankfulness that allows you to see the gifts of their companionship.

True Life

The passage of time reminds me that I live in a human frame. I have come to know true life is life lived out in the living Christ by the Word of the living God. While beginning to try and live the spiritual life, I am constantly faced with my humanness.

True life is the holy transformation of life to the spiritual. True life is eternal life lived out in the present and is spiritual lived out in the flesh. The passage of time has no substantial effect and matters of the flesh are subdued for the one living a life of grace and peace.

He Had Waited

He had waited all this time
Through sickness, doubt, and rehabilitation.
Knowing all the while that if
I could catch a glimpse of Jesus,
I would be His and He mine.

He Has Saved

It is the fact He has saved
Me that humbles me.

Falling Short

Falling short in this earthly home
Can make one seek in any
Direction on a painful road until
The heart learns of and trusts
A saving grace that transfigures
It to new birth. Only then does
The heart find heavenly rest.

My Will

I am here by His will.
So, shouldn't my will yield to His?

Home

Home is not where you are,
It is who you are with.

My Hope

My hope is not based on my feeling,
My hope is based on Him.

I Have Found

I have found that
I am found.

Stillness and Silence

Stillness and silence.
Deafness and confusion.
A yearning to hear; sounds to discern.

Then the recognition of music and
Hearing the notes.
Listening in new ways.
Passive listening in quiet moments.
Active listening in singing.

The sound of silence through
The confusion of deafness to
The gift of singing.

Just As I Am

The Lord loves me just as I am.
Shouldn't I accept myself as
What I am, who I am
And whose I am?

Taking Your Place

By God's Son taking your place on the cross of shame,
Something new happens to you if you only come to see it.
God's intention is to let you find Him and by the emptied
Cross save you, remake you, and adopt you as His own.
He will give you His Kingdom, protect you from harm and
Love you ceaselessly. You will begin anew the
Life He has given you with His Holy Spirit as your guide.

If We Had a Pen

If we had a pen in our hands
Would we not write of His glory
And the love He gave to us
By His son in prose, poetry
And song?

The Door to Heaven's Staircase

Your own recognition of your need for repentance offers you

An opportunity to knock at the door of forgiveness.

Your knock will assuredly cause this door to open.

As the door opens to you, you discover,

As so many have before you,

The first step to a staircase to the realms of Heaven.

Climbing the staircase to points above

Requires faith in the One beyond.

For you to reach its highest step,

The slope of the staircase, its number of stairs

And the gradual rise of each step has been made

Just right for you to exercise and strengthen your heart.

As each step of the staircase disappears behind you,

You come into view of your Heavenly King and Savior

When you reach the final stair.

You find yourself upon firm foundation anchored in

Unconditional love and acceptance

Which transforms your heart's condition immediately.

You begin to explore within this expansive surrounding space

Of peace and grace and feel a silent warm loving embrace.

Your own sigh of relief signals an emotional release

That leaves you with a calm never before experienced.

As you rest, you realize this:

For the first time, you are home with your God.

The door that had opened before you

And the staircase at the start of your climb

Were made possible by the Cross of His Son.
There, at its entranceway, the door, door frame,
Threshold, and staircase had been lovingly
Built by the Carpenter who died many years ago.
He did this for the expressed purpose for you to knock,
Climb, discover, and rest in the eternal arms of His Father.
The Carpenter is somewhere close by.
When He appears to you, thank Him.

Everything Beautiful in Its Time

> *"11 He hath made every thing beautiful in its time: also he hath set the world in their heart, so that no man can find out the work that God maketh from the beginning to the end." (Ecclesiastes 3:11)*

A loon on the surface of water causing a ripple.

The gallop of a stallion causing mud to fly.

A rainbow's appearance amid a gentle rainstorm.

The yawn of a tiny newborn.

Droplets of water resting within a spider's web.

A nip in the autumn air.

A butterfly taken to flight off milkweed.

A doe posing in forested trees.

The smell of the nutty fragrance of fallen leaves.

A frog on its stony perch in the undergrowth.

A clear night's moonlight reflected off lake water.

The slap of wave upon shore in sliding step.

The stillness of high mountain snow.

The approaching winter with wood fires burning.

A line of birds sitting at rest on a wire.

The departure of hummingbirds at the window feeder.

The play of small children in the rustle of fallen leaves.

A squirrel sitting erect, munching nuts.

An eagle flying free.

Blooming lilies in a small pond.

Geese flying skyward in their pattern.

The gleeful face of a child embracing a pumpkin.

The bells that call out for a time of prayer.

The anticipation of a night star in the East

Coming to rest at God's command over Bethlehem.

To one's eyes, God's orchestral symphony of living activity

Appears as a balanced kaleidoscope dancing across the earth.

These are indeed gifts of God touching our senses.

God's beauty in the time of life if only for a moment

Yet remembered eternally. "We give thanks for

God's creative force from the tidal mark

To the timberline." (Rev. Phil White)[*]

---

[*] from Rev. Phil White's sermon.

Where There Is No Shadow

In this life, though we walk with
Limited understanding of the valley
Of the shadow of death, we know that we are with God
And we move and have our being in Him.
God's Light shines with no shadow.
God's Love holds with no condition.
For with God, death has been swallowed up
As evidenced by the resurrection of His Son.
In this life, we experience shadows.
Yet we have been given the hope and promise
Of His resurrection and new life in Jesus.
With the bestowing of the Holy Spirit upon us,
Shadows disappear and His eternal life appears before us.
God's Light stands and shines upon us here and now,
And His love carries us through this life
To His while His Light shines all about.

Strangers

If you are going to love your neighbor as yourself, you must love strangers as your neighbors, too. Be a neighbor to a stranger. In this way they will become your neighbor and you will have more friends around the globe.

Rhyme Your Life

Rhyme your life with the love of the Lord
And you will find that you have a relationship with His Father.
Rhyme your life with the will of the Lord
And you will champion it for His purposes.
Rhyme your life with His following
And you will find His way for your life.
Rhyme your life with Jesus' mercy for you from His cross
And you will find that you are forgiven beyond measure, and
Rhyme your life with Jesus' resurrection
And you will find that your life is renewed in Him.

MLK Jr. and Reconciliation

Heavenly Father, thank you for giving me the life and the space to believe and pray that we are a forgiven people because of your Son Jesus for what He did for us on the cross. We are a loved people shown by the mercy of your Son's choice to obey you on our behalf. We are a reconciled people who through your Son's sacrifice for us care deeply about our relationship with you, a relationship you have given us at great cost. You have given all we need to live in peace in your Kingdom which is not of this world but is on this earth to be sure because of the birth and death of your Son.

We know your Kingdom that teaches hope, grace, peace, and love will live in the hearts of all who dare to love and live on earth caring deeply for the world in which they live. The late Reverend Dr. Martin Luther King, Jr. knew this about your Kingdom and dared with love and the audacity of hope, and Heavenly purpose to bring peace among peoples and race in the United States. He was your child living in your Kingdom. He was on earth, a witness to your Son's message of reconciliation and forgiveness that was purchased on your Son's cross for all and with all the strength of his conviction, he brought that witness forward into the public discourse of this country. He had your purposes for the people of this country in the palm of his hand.

Today, more than fifty years after his death, hatred seems so close and our peoples are so divided as if we could forget and dismiss or could not have known who we witnessed the man Reverend King to be. Have we learned nothing from that time so as to forget why Jesus came to set us free from the shackles of our own bondage with each other and as a nation? Will we learn Jesus' lesson to live in peace with one another?

For all time, Jesus will be our best example and the deep hope of our hearts for reconciliation to flourish among the people of the United States. Because of this, in time, your love will be seen through us if we, like Reverend King, have the courage and audacity as he did to step forward to express the will and purpose of your Kingdom through Christ Jesus. For our part, we need to be able to express our shared faith with other faiths in this country to repel hate and embrace love for the common good and civil discourse.

Environment of Faith

Mountaintops are for blessed sermons,
And clouds are for transfigurations.

Seas are for deliverance,
And rivers are for the beginning of new life.

Valleys are for coming to terms with shadows,
And deserts are for overcoming.

Rain is for awakenings,
And bushes are for burning.

Rocks are for new waters,
And hills are for light and sacrifice.

Gardens are for joy and sorrow,
And trees are for forgiveness.

Rainbows are for promise,
And stars are for the guiding.

Grass is for earthly time,
And lilies are for grace.

Fish are for the journey to follow,
And doves are for Spirit.

Stable animals, sheep and birds
Are for lessons and story.

Stones rolled away are for resurrections,
And Heaven is for home.

Jesus' hand is for the grasping,
And our journey is with Him
On this road of life.

250 Ways to Love the Lord

Believe in God.

Believe in Jesus.

Have faith in Him.

Hope in the Lord.

Praise Him.

Serve Him.

Love your God with all your heart.

Love your neighbors and your enemies,

And love yourself.

Forgive one another.

Humbly walk with your God.

Pray without ceasing.

Seek His Kingdom.

Invite all to the table.

Hold each other up.

Keep His commandments.

Hold high the cross.

Hear the good news.

Be anxious for nothing.

Lean not on your own understanding.

Consider the lilies of the field,

Let life be free of worry.

Be transformed.

Run the race set before us.

Look to the perfecter of our faith.

Lay aside the world's weight.

Let us be glad today.

Do not lose heart.

Sing a new song.

Open a gate for others.

Wait upon the Lord.

Be glad in this day that God has made.

Be still before the Lord.

Cultivate joy.

Walk in His statutes.

Feed His people.

Do not hide your light.

Accept what is offered.

Do not flaunt your wealth,

Give some of it away.

Believe in the sanctity of life.

Marvel at the mystery of life.

Put your hand in His.

Be undisturbed by the weight of the world.

Let God work in your life.

Let God work in others.

Expect tribulation.

Give it to the Lord.

Bless others on their way.

Care for relationships.

Stand on His firm foundation.

Heed His message.

Follow Him.

Offer gifts to Him.

Repent.

Rejoice.

Act graciously.

Hold onto what is good.

Turn the other cheek.

Be a good listener.

Help the afflicted.

Be joyful in the face of trials.

Strengthen the faith of others.

Lift a spirit.

Spread goodwill.

Preach.

Be at peace with one another.

Turn swords into plowshares.

Turn spears into pruning hooks.

Feed the hungry.

Supply a need.

Care for the homeless.

Care for the disenfranchised.

Relieve pain.

Be expectant.

Offer hope.

Offer grace.

Light a path for others.

Give of your time.

Give of your resources.

Lead others to the Lord.

Hold tightly to Him.

Calm a storm.

Show compassion.

Give assurance.

Trust in Him.

Coexist.

Share the broken bread.

Share the cup.

Give someone a smile.

Mend a quarrel.

Apologize for a wrong.

Resolve anger.

Keep your promises.

Keep your commitments.

Encourage hearts for the Lord.

Accept that which cannot be changed.

Recognize that which is dark.

Seek common understanding.

Accept others.

See possibilities.

Know that miracles happen.

Live with honorable intentions.

Be truthful to yourself.

Be truthful to others.

Walk in the light.

Befriend someone.

Include another.

Develop friendships.

Accept differences.

Have wonder for God's world.

Put your hand in His.

Think rightly.

Practice humility.

Explore God's creation.

Accept the present moment.

Don't fret about tomorrow.

Remember Him.

Share the good news.

Gather with friends.

Share in His abundance.

Shout for joy.

Search for the lost.

Point the way to Him.

Welcome strangers.

Carry another's burdens.

Put your burdens on Him.

Walk in another man's shoes.

Do not bear grudges.

Be in the Light.

Live from the deepest part of yourself.

Give the love that is in your heart.

Be truthful before the Lord.

Be true to His Word.

Show mercy.

Spread goodwill.

Kindle the Spirit.

Let the Lord make the way.

Make peace.

Bind up wounds.

Read the Bible.

Ponder God's Word.

Speak plainly of God.

Be kind.

Release the captives.

Be contrite.

Give alms.

Teach others.

Do not boast.

Turn around.

Be honest.

Speak truthfully.

Live simply.

Do justice.

Be an example.

Show patience.

Kneel before the Lord.

Be forthright.

Believe in God.

Believe in Jesus.

Comfort.

Be steadfast.

Honor your mother and father.

Trust.

Be gentle.

Walk the narrow way.

Lift up.

Have God's perspective.

Be slow to anger.

Judge not.

Offer a hand.

Prepare the way.

Share the life.

Speak the truth.

Speak sincerely.

Count your blessings.

Give of your abundance.

Accept yourself as God's child.

Appreciate beauty.

Obey His commands.

Accept criticism.

Raise hopes.

Live in harmony.

Practice selflessness.

Do not deceive.

Treat yourself forgivingly.

Glorify the Lord.

And acknowledge His ways.

Be a steward of the earth.

Be kind to animals.

Be true to your word.

Give a hand.

Give a hug.

Give direction.

Give hope where there seems none.

Hold fast to the truth.

Offer assistance.

Study scripture.

Read with God's light.

Support the faint hearted.

Lift up the weak.

Render no one evil for evil.

Offer aid to the infirm.

Let the Lord's light shine.

Find common ground.

Hope for the very best in others.

Keep holy the Sabbath.

Sing a new song to the Lord.

Promote conversation about the Lord.

Draw circles that draw people in.

Accept what is offered.

Give some of what you have away.

Believe in the sanctity of Life.

Know that Jesus is the answer.

Mend a quarrel.

Seek out a forgotten friend.

Dismiss a suspicion,

Replace it with trust.

Give a soft answer.

Encourage youth.

Keep a promise.

Find time for someone else.

Forgo a grudge.

Forgive an enemy.

Apologize when you are wrong.

Try to understand.

Think first of someone else.

Appreciate.

Be gentle.

Laugh a little,

Laugh a little more.

Welcome a stranger.

Speak your love,

Speak it again,

Speak it still again.

I Am Carved on The Palm of His Hand

A doctor diagnosed me with Schizophrenia.

Jesus saw the confusion.

The doctor gave me counseling and medicine.

Jesus gave me hope,

Connected me with His Father's love,

And taught me about His way and truth of life.

Over time the Schizophrenia symptoms subsided.

Jesus said, "Your faith has made you well."

A second doctor diagnosed me with Multiple Myeloma.

Jesus saw the condition.

And said to me, "Follow me."

"Your faith has made you well."

Jesus has diagnosed me as His Father's child.

Jesus has diagnosed me as God's adopted son.

Jesus has diagnosed me as a good and faithful servant.

Jesus has blessed me with courage and grace.

Jesus has steadied me with patience.

Jesus is with me in all manner of trials.

And when loss appears, Jesus reassures me:

"There is no loss in God."

There is room for me at the foot of the cross.

In the stillness, Jesus is the answer to prayer.

After every storm, Jesus offers sweet words of joy.

He has given me the gifts of Love, Hope, Joy, and Grace.

His will is unchanging and His mind is on me.

He is my redeemer and my savior.

And He is my joy.

Jesus has diagnosed me with joyful laughter.

Jesus has diagnosed me with a peaceful heart.

He has blessed me with kindness,

And reassured me in times of trouble

That He will always be with me,

Holding me carved on the palm of His hand.

For me, in the beauty of the universe, there is

Nothing lovelier than a relationship with God

Through the Son.

The Mind of Christ

Going from the distorted thought (Schizophrenia) to stable, single-mindedness by discovering the mind of God.

My Unending Joy

Nowhere Else to Go

Many years ago, I went off to Jesus because I had nowhere else to go.

Realizing

I have come to realize this:
Once I came to know Jesus
And realized His purpose for me,
I saw that my celebration of
The birth, life, death, and resurrection of the
Son of God is the overwhelming joy in my life.
When I celebrate this with others, our lives have
Deeper meaning together.

The Miracle of This Life

To become separated in darkness,
To search and catch a glimpse,
There to discover my profound need for the Lord,
To seek him in truth,
To find him
And then to discover and experience
That I am never to be separated
From the Savior nor the depth of
His light, love and grace in Holy embrace
Is truly the miracle of this life.

Healed in the Ocean of God's Love

It happened one night:
A soul awakened to the fright of a new reality—
Broken and scared, inside and out,
Beached on a new shoreline of
Distraction and pain.

Not knowing an ocean of God's love with its tides
Was nearby, the soul lay upon the sand bed,
The sharpness of its deeply injured brokenness.

Looming in a long afternoon, a violent storm carried a
Turbulent wave of water reaching the soul
Rhythmically covering it with soothing foam and spray.

Newness of torment, suffering and anguish was present
For the one covered in water, cool and moist.
God was now at work reviving that soul
As beach glass is rounded when jumbled
On that shoreline by stone and wave of life.

As time passed, the soul was ushered to new waters by
Raindrop and shower, moving it closer ever to the ocean's edge
For the healing touch of God's love.

Finally reaching near in the vast arms of God in wet repose,
The wounded soul cried out "Abba Father": the splash of relief
And the sinking deep.

The soul being rounded and smoothed like beach glass,
Day in and day out; the sharpness of its pain transformed

By God's word and the example of living water.

Over many years, living water healed and carried that soul
Far away from that shoreline of distraction and pain giving it
Example and lesson, story and psalm to live by in that ocean
Of God's love.

And God's ocean of love went about setting that healed soul aright
For its new life well past its fright of brokenness and pain.

Joy of Life

I have found that the joy of life is this:

To learn of and accept the Lord's will and way for me;
A perfect gift for me to realize my eternal link
With my majestic Father, His Son and Holy Spirit.

A gift He has ordained by His hand
Given to me in specific Sonship;
A gift for me to understand
At His teaching in His good time and way.

A blessing, honor, and glorious gift for me
To grow as a child He loves
Into the Christian He refines in order
For me to see my purpose in His.

My Shepherd

The Shepherd is my Lord who guides me along

His path of righteousness to bring my life

Into focus and upon my reflection, gives my life

Meaning and purpose. He stands beside me to offer me

His peace for the situation at hand;

His grace for the moment; and

His love to sustain.

Come down this path with me

And you will find Faith, Hope and Joy

Just as I have. It has made all the difference in my step.

And it will make a difference in yours.

You and I will be restored to walk with Him down

His path that has no end.

Come along and you will find the life you

Have been looking for;

The one He has always wanted you to have.

The Joy I Have Found in Jesus

There was a time when the conditions

Of my life overwhelmed me and loneliness

Was my constant companion. My loneliness

Caused me to turn to Jesus.

And in my praise of Jesus, I discovered the gift of song.

In my singing, I discerned my voice.

In my voice, I discovered myself.

In accepting myself, I found a life with others.

And in accepting others, I discovered the

Loveliness of the human family;

And its conditions—conditions, yes, of

Loneliness, depression, separation, fear,

Anxiety and poverty. I know now these conditions

Can be defeated when presented to Jesus.

Let me be an example. I pray!

So that my joy that I find in Jesus may be complete.

Loving Him

Loving me, the Lord delivered me through
My worst fear while I did not know Him
To bring me to my greatest joy, knowing and loving Him.

Christ Had The Key

Many years ago, Christ had the key
to the prison I was in.
He has unlocked it for good.

Bibliography

1.   White, Rev. Philip. <u>Sermon</u>. Rock Spring Congregational, UCC, Arlington, Virginia.

2.   Austin, Rev. Jack. <u>Sermon</u>. First Christian Church Falls Church, Falls Church, Virginia.

3.   King James Version. American Bible Society. New York. 1611 (Public Domain)

Author Bio

Wendel L. Miser

I grew up in the same home in New England with my brother Jim. I was, however, preoccupied with my twin brother, Andy, in our formative years and through high school. It was in high school that I met my wife, Mary, marrying her in September 1972, after finishing at Cornell College in Mt. Vernon, Iowa in June of 1973.

I received a Master of Science degree from the University of Illinois in 1975, after studying Zoology and Limnology. After graduate school, I worked with Mary's father in his painting business before accepting a position in the Office of Solid Waste at the United States Environmental Protection Agency in Washington, D.C. in 1977.

I began with their program of pesticide disposal for a short time and then became a project officer, managing the program side for the Agency's contract office. Working with the contract officer, I helped the staff with contract pre-award and post-award requirements for their work. In that capacity, I was involved for 23 years in the development of a nationwide hazardous waste management program. Subsequently, I moved to the Office's municipal waste program that was promoting recycling and sustainability programs at the time.

While not at work during the latter half of my career, I became interested in singing. For the better part of 20 years, I was involved with the New Dominion Chorale and the National Men's Chorus in the Washington, D.C. area. The New Dominion Chorale featured works by the Great Masters, while the National Men's Chorus showcased works specially arranged by the music director for the Chorus. Memorable concerts were given at the National Cathedral and the Kennedy Center as well as the National Gallery of Art, Washington, D.C. For six years, I served on the Board of Directors of the National Men's Chorus, assisting with grant activities.

I live with my wife in Arlington, Virginia and our two cats, Linus and Madeleine. We attend church regularly in Falls Church, Virginia. I have kept a faith-based journal for 38 years. In overcoming schizophrenia and finding joy, I have entered full participation in life.

Author Bio

James S. Miser, MD

I grew up on the East Coast of the United States with my father, mother, two younger twin brothers, and a younger sister, spending the majority of time in New England. My father was a mathematician with a PhD in this field, and he was an operations research and systems analysis professional.

My mother had a Master of Science degree in Child Development; she spent most of our formative years caring for us as we grew and developed. We were a normal family and could not know what was to befall Wendel at age 28.

I am a Pediatric Hematologist and Oncologist and have taken care of children with cancer and blood diseases for almost 50 years. I received a Bachelor of Arts degree from Dartmouth College in

Hanover, New Hampshire, in 1969, majoring in Religion. While there, I also was the director of the college's acapella singing group.

In the summers during high school and college, I taught tennis to children. Although I intended to be a mathematician, I decided to spend my life working with children and entered Dartmouth Medical School with the intention to be a pediatrician. I subsequently transferred to the University of Washington in Seattle, Washington, where I received a Doctor of Medicine in 1973 and trained in Pediatrics and Pediatric Hematology and Oncology.

At the beginning of my experience of caring for children with cancer, I accepted the Lord Jesus Christ as Lord and Savior of my life. This has been an important relationship for me since that time. I have worked as a Pediatric Hematologist/Oncologist at: Ohio State University; the National Institutes of Health; Mayo Clinic; the University of Washington, where I was granted the position of Professor of Pediatrics; and City of Hope National Medical Center, where I was Chairman of Pediatrics.

I also served as President and Chief Medical Officer at City of Hope National Medical Center as it developed a comprehensive cancer center.

I have authored more than 100 manuscripts and book chapters. I worked as medical director and served as Chairman of the American Board of Directors of a child rescue organization—Christian Salvation Service, in Taipei, Taiwan, serving children and women. During this time, I was also Chair Professor of Pediatrics at Taipei Medical University, where I was challenged to develop a Pediatric Hematology/Oncology program for the University.

I also served as Chairman of the Board of Directors of a Christian High School in southern California and currently serve as Chairman of the Board of Directors of a nonprofit organization supporting children with cancer and their families.

My wife Angela and I have adopted 10 children, many with significant challenges. I live in Wales with my wife and five of the children. I enjoy walking, reading, playing tennis, and singing. I attend church with my wife in the Church of Wales. The mission of my life has been to serve children, both personally and professionally, especially those with significant challenges in their lives.

I have been close to my brother, Wendel, in his journey with schizophrenia and shared the initial horror, the subsequent anxiety of the ups and downs of his experience, and now the joy of his overcoming.

It has been a privilege to travel his journey and to write this book with him.